MW01196689

BURN
IT
DOWN

BURN IT DOWN

POEMS

KATIE BYRUM

FORKLIFT_BOOKS

FORKLIFT BOOKS EDITION, February 2015

Copyright © 2015 by Katie Byrum
All rights reserved. Printed in the United States of America.

ISBN 978-0-9903082-0-1

Edited by Matt Hart
Book and cover design by Eric Appleby

For a complete listing of titles, please visit
www.forkliftbooks.com

For more on this book, visit
www.h-ngm-n.com/burnitdown

an imprint of

H_NGM_N
B O O K S
www.h-ngm-nbks.com

For Owen, who brought me to the edge
and for Smeltz, who brought me back.

PROLOGUE

after Catullus

Whether I will be gadabout, vagabond, magnet,
or dig down to the innermost spot where the core wound
     booms,
as Pacific surf hits black cliffs;

whether I will fret and go so inward only a hard shake
can wake me, or fling myself so far into belligerence
they have to yank me by the hair to bring me back;

even should I dream of a house with a turret
under which a bed purrs to have me in it
like hobo gals outside who rub their drunken sideskins
against the grimy legs of their men, my friends stay true.

As for that boy, I'd have him know this one truth:
I hope his kitchen crew applauds his every move, that he
     finds some peace
in sous vide or shaved fennel, tattooed ladies or the post-
     shift beer
that leaves him flat on his back and almost foaming at the
     mouth—

May he never feel the right to touch my arm with
     tenderness
after such time's passed, or know the names

of flowers I've bought from the farmer's market,
pinch them and wink in the way I always liked,

since I've made plans to bring them to my new love's room
and put them in glass on the nightstand, and my arm has
    gone numb
from clutching at their cut stems,
and only barely wants to feel his fingerprints again.

TABLE OF CONTENTS

Notes & Acknowledgments

About the Author

"More is happening out there than we are aware of.
It is possibly due to some unknown direful circumstance."

—Edward Gorey, "L'heure Bleue"

BURN IT DOWN

just home from work my hair stringy
and ketchup on my shoes
found you shirtless with a table saw
going apeshit on a two-by-four
watching British sitcoms and laughing
I held the frame you
nailed in place we worked
quietly beside each other
nails between our teeth hammering down
the stretched fabric blue
with gingko leaves I folded
the corners down like birthday presents
you stepped back squinting
it was crooked just slightly
two inches over
up a little on the right
well voilà aren't we
just something this room has
sawdust over everything
and footprints through it
proving you were here
I didn't want to sweep it up
such a fine sheen over everything

PARADISE

"Don't leave me stranded here
I can't get used to this lifestyle"

—Talking Heads, "(Nothing But) Flowers"

Life in Suburbia quickly became lukewarm.
It was Easter, and as is the custom
we put Peeps in the microwave, watched them swell and spin
like junior prom, seeing stars until they almost burst—
America!

Who here hasn't failed
to banish the old jingles?
This is the parking lot of my discontent:
Starbucks, blank blank, black tar, blank blank,
Chick-fil-A with extra sauce, et cetera,
We all know about having
too much of a good thing.

I washed a Xanax down with coffee and felt perfectly status quo.
There was a pleasant chill though the sun was shining,
I looked into it and I almost felt—

No. I bought three things for dinner. White packages inside
    white boxes.
In the parking lot there was a great expanse. I forget what it
    was for
but there was caution tape around it.

Shopping cart chain gangs rattle their bones;
between guardrails, the highway moans.
Plastic water bottle crackle. Shitty plastic bag shuffle.
Whoever you are, promise you'll pardon our mess.

CAN'T BE TOO CAREFUL

Whosoever had a seasonal hell, this was certainly it:
the brother of whatever my peace got snagged on, passing—
the sudden turn of a careless word into an argument,
drinks diluting in the jar while complaints rehearsed
in the mirror. So I ran; my mind turned panoramic.
I was 360° of apology, all day long I was apology!
Sorries to the grocer, the mailman, the sad flesh at the back
of the old woman's arm. It got so I hardly had to make
    mistakes at all;
I nipped them in the bud with my endless *forgive me*, and
    stopped going outside
for fear I'd brush a stranger's hand with mine or step on a
    bug unwittingly.

It was written: the lonesome curse of the only child, who
    worries,
who thinks only of herself and her world inside the
    apartment, flooded
with gray light and hammer noise from under next door's
    blue tarps.
Cancels that mythology, she does, and rides away upon a
    swift horse.

CHRISTMAS STORY

I fucked up tomorrow 'cause I loved today so well
coming home half drunk with the sky going orange
around the city joggers, business faces rushing past
while I stumbled into the day full of holiday cheer
I bought a Christmas tree recklessly
I couldn't help it he was a Frenchman
his name was Emmanuel for Chrissakes like a fool
I stood there avoiding my bedtime
haggling as usual getting the story out
Americans he said have a real syntactic problem
everything is like something else
he was like, it was like, like, like—this tree is a nice one
I used to take too much cocaine he said
I was raised on a farm we had terrific cows
sometimes I think this life is too much but then—cows
No, horses are not for me their eyes
make them too much like drunks
they can't look you straight in the eye

MODEL AIRPLANE

you held a model airplane
upside-down by its Styrofoam tail
not looking anyone in the eye
where did you go
when you were small
inside that plane?

ROAD TRIP

for Smeltz

Train landscape comes forward
a red blur to my left
I get a shoelace-in-an-escalator feeling
little pieces coming in from where: oh you sleepers wake

This poem can make you happier
all its reds and blues

Today I crossed two rivers
and I'm not finished yet:
say "Susquehanna" in your accent-of-steel
armed with a "bag of Americana"
all my bitches   Dickinson
Frost and hard cider:
tastes like the earth it came from

you grape whisperer   little red storyteller
everything wants to talk   you have to learn how to listen
shoe clack and
gum pop and the truest word I know: OR
some words still keep their hooks in me
like when the poet stopped his reading to say to me
I see you   yes its true
when you cut me I bleed, I'm not sure
it's possible to not live this way

even the headlines know it:
"The Perils of Uncertainty"

I wish this day were colder
have to go back to the source:
how one woman's creek
is another woman's river
wide glinting body   you take it all away
we go: with a feeling of fashionable danger

yes the road rises to meet me
at my stupid country places:
Bob Evans Max & Erma's Cracker Barrel
I become an ig-no-ray-moose in an old rocking chair
Pittsburgh in a flattering light   Ohio
with its desolate flats
and burned-out barns and sky
with a promise at the edges

A NIGHT LIKE THIS

They love a night like this.
Obliteration's wild and quiet rush,
the star-blown snow
so beautiful it makes them stupid.

—Paul Violi, "Buckaroo"

Amped up, off the clock but still in uniform:
in slip-proof shoes that love
when a crack in the routine opens
and these two find the night

dragging them by the hand,
pouring out tequila shots they will drink
down an ice luge dusted with crushed-up Doritos—
a little sloshy now, rushing out

into a night like this, past Doppler voices,
hectic plaid and yellow cabs, the lights
so red and white insistent and slurry they shut their eyes
and tumble back into the star-blown snow

and lie there dwarfed into silence by cold and stars,
belly up to the sky and reaching
for the other's hand in a drunk and snowy dark
so beautiful it makes them stupid.

HEART TATTOO

Today's apology for last night's disaster
your hand through a wall   drunk and trying to erase
don't get like that please   come back from there

just this last time   we were going to kiss
we did kiss and I closed the door

But I hear through walls:
the woman who tattoos you
calls on the phone
a buzzing in the other room

The new art came in stages
each sitting you grew new colors
and more of you disappeared
in shades and outlines
that did not belong to me

Her hair trailing down
over you, with needles

I watched it grow   knowing the feeling
the heart coming out of your chest
a red design that took the place
of what you had left to give

AMERICA, IF YOU WANT ME, YOU CAN FIND ME AT THE BAR

"Good morning, I'm not drunk and I'm never in a hurry
Don't mind the green sparkles on my face
It's the pixie I made love to at 3 a.m.
She was so goddamn good-looking I couldn't say no"

I try to give a word for how you make me feel and that word is—
fucker

The TV on. Like a weird bird I say whatever
the characters say, I believe in anything
my director tells me: just let go
my delirious two sides, let my two lives crash: fine
I just hope someone is listening

Today I called in sick
I wanted out of my life for just one day
When I leapt I broke it, my minutes
I gave you like a present that mattered

If I keep my sword by my side
I will want to slay something
In real life you are beautiful
I didn't leave enough time to tell you
how I wanted the walls to come down

FORECAST

I can't make my comeback in this
less auspicious environment
the tall man in the bookstore   great impostor
stealing the seat I was ready to sit in
I get tired of fighting passive wars
it's not worth my time   what's your name?

Today: a chain reaction
with good views of the sky,
mostly no one looks out the window,
just generally aware of the rough outline of clouds

    I love you best when your back is turned
    I love you best when you're in the other room

Full of questions
I wish you'd listen but when you do
I can't quite—
there was something important about clouds

I become like you   an early riser
stumbling into the day haphazard
as is customary, no coffee no umbrella but
I brought a book called *Rain* it is a fine
yellow book it fits right in my bag
I can feel it when I walk

the wet sidewalk   gingko leaves everywhere
children calling each other archaic names:
Hazel   Agnes   Henry   et cetera
everything is making a comeback

WHAT HAPPENS IN THIS TOWN STAYS IN THIS TOWN

This one I couldn't hold: he'd gone bottom-fishing
in his own head, deciding what of me to keep.
He finally surfaced in a flurry of bubbles:
I said strange weather ever since you got back

and his eyes said yes: his eyes were everywhere
cast on my skin, which could feel
what his fingerprints were thinking.

Through rainclothes our blood made a lazy agreement
and my skin began its dream through his hands,
through their myth of Middle America, their invention

of prairie songs and rough timber. In his palms
I saw maps of red dust and rivers—
saw them pressed to me and lifting
to show their lines in arrows on my skin.

My blood in barrel knots, I was caught in his ring of prayer
and so turned to the gods of the lake: let me absorb
some geography of elsewhere, mark the crossroads of two rivers
on the small of my back. On my ribs, the saloon's swinging door.

DUMB LUCK

Saturday, we've overslept
I'm going back in to wrestle your dream:
won't you wake up love, there is so much
I wanted to tell you, I pull the covers from between us
find the place to wake you & touch

are you still
sleeping—suddenly stranger,
my heart pounds   so hard the room is shaking or maybe—
your leg is twitching what's
happening?   the door
gets indecisive on its hinges
a piece of the earth slips past itself

earthquakes sudden as panic attacks
strong love or restlessness
the blinds sway gently right and left
the world's reminder   it's still here, still
moving beneath us:
a sudden failure of the forces that keep things from moving
taking issue with form   with being asked
to stay there lie down be round

nothing like a rattle to remind us that we're here
yes: it's dangerous to be a human being

when the curtains stop swaying and the plates settle
the neighborhood reacts like any Tuesday:
yelling and car alarms, business as usual,
a return to making love—
always things moving, always sleep to fight off,
the dream-fray unraveling when I doze off and dream you
and wake surprised to see you're still right here

stupid love
dumb luck
this round and rumbling earth

SEVEN DEADLY SINS: NEW YORK EDITION

You wouldn't believe
the emergencies I've walked past—
I've refused change to beggars
with leftovers burning a hole in my bag,
I have snarled at fat men
who called me beautiful,
feigned sick in the face of birthdays—
too far on the train, too far—felt lust
crackle in a subway car: hands touching
on the pole; I let them, I let them—
I have plugged my ears, shoved tourists
& given the dirtiest looks:
oh you who eat tuna on the train,
oh you holder-of-doors, the god-sized
width of your strollers, I am sorry, I was wrathful;
I have eyeballed the shoes of countless
handsome women & let a competition
grow in me, I have stolen from the lost
& found & picked flowers
I did not grow
& as for the woman
whose headscarf bobbed with *Christ*
has risen—I bowed my head
& went back to my book

ONE NIGHTSTAND

Take this syringe, for example.
Certain methods of extracting love may be easier,
but they won't be as effective.

Instead of trying to talk to you, I wrap my idea of love
around a china bone: I am getting tired
and no one will respond. But also, to what?

Things keep disappearing from the nightstand,
like my whole removable life grows legs
and walks off while I'm sleeping.

I don't know where anything goes, but we can find out
tonight, over packs and packs of cigarettes. I'll take the extras—
I don't mean—is there more wine?

Oh god I am trying to find a place.
A sign that shows good things are going to happen
and we can have whatever we want, for free.

In any case, I have to remember to breathe,
and keep at least one surprise. Like the next morning,
when something will vanish that isn't small.

RESTRAINT

It's a hard situation to escape. Just ask the captain:
My seatbelt is low and tight across my lap,
and I secure my own mask before helping others.

After hearty chicken dinners, my uncle
unbuckles his belt. I go outside
to ogle the stars; I complain of night blindness

to get a prescription. Now I suck on weed lollies to calm me,
skateboard down the city's tallest hills
while my sober friends wheeze in my tailwinds. In Russia,

I'm forbidden to sit on curbs in winter, no matter
how late the bus, for local superstition has it
that doing so may freeze my future children.

Who needs offspring? I'll heart NY instead. On Broadway,
drag queens, shellacked like Fabergé eggs, are still
     somebody's baby.
Even I was ornate, like a figure in a souvenir snow globe.

In college, we named our bong
The Punisher. I dropped so much acid,
I floated weightless to the top

of the Dean's List. What color is your parachute?
And how sure are you
that when you jump it will open?

In the home office, library binding has a certain masochistic
    appeal.
This year, I'll bring you home and trim the Christmas tree
with caution tape. When I give the grand tour, I'll make sure
    to tell you:

In case of emergency, break this glass.

Don't ask how I'm doing,
just see me, how I brace myself
against the kitchen counter,
how I hold on with two hands
to stay anchored in the world
of real things: crumbs, ants,
the chocolates I slipped in your pocket
partly to please you, partly to keep them from myself—
you are the only one who might decipher
my head's hieroglyphics   but:
do you see me—am I fine—
do I seem fine to you?

Tell us how we are doing!
We want to hear what you think!

CHECK, PLEASE

Garçon, finish your spiel or I might keel over!
About this dinner there is nothing I trust.
Barbacoa, tequila, and a blue-eyed barkeep.
I like sweet, but not *too* sweet—
nothing's free in this world. A round on the house
gets him muttering; over chicken, his suspicions
become war. Empathetic oh-honey looks from the staff
and I'm thinking, I beg you to ruin this:
somebody, spilled wine, maître d', anybody,
escape me to the powder room!
Another such victory and I am undone.
How much more careful can I get?
Am I doomed to fog up the mirror again?
By candlelight our talk has turned sullen,
turned to trench warfare. So okay, I see it, I'll go now:
I love you stopped having the right of way.
My best intentions suffocate: but at least they can admit
they've won the battle but lost the war.

BIG BUCK HUNTER

Game night, I go stag
avoiding the empty apartment
the corner where I got jumped

Kamikaze birthday shot
compliments of the regulars

Jam coins in the slot
Get Ready, Hunter Hero
You killed a cow!

Burn notice: today started out
crying in the boiler room
ends in flames at Hank's Saloon

Red plastic kickback
mallard duck murder
Perfect sites   Perfect streak

I shoot the geese the deer the helpless squirrels
the birthday boy, his girlfriend too
& every Wild Turkey in this place

Triple Ram
Fuck you, majestic steed
I am having a very bad day

AT THE END OF THE HIGHLINE

Under the flight path
beside the water
helicopters and the highway
one neon jogger stops to ask
if I have the time
clouds drip down a dusty sky
a rent-a-cop rolls slowly by
I try not to be skittish
though the noises are foreign
blades that slash the dark
I try not to be alone
too often these days
if I can I will sit with my back to the wall
it's a comfort to know that nobody's behind me

up on the Highline
staring at everyone staring back
in strangers' pictures I will be small
and secondary scenery
to see the city clearly you have to be
at some remove why
this is true I can't
quite say up here I don't look
at dead winter grasses but
in the backlit windows
strangers move red curtains

someone watches in a striped sweater
a maid vacuums the same spot twice
are we to understand that distance
as a perfected art
going and going over it

long distance runners go
the same path each time, blood
pounding in their ears they
monitor their heart rates
on sculpted watches
that light up the dark

I can see everyone from here
coming into clarity
on gravity—sometimes kind
in keeping us here
other times letting us fall

A VIPER I FOUND

dreamt of slow rivers
dreamt I had electric hair
slept on your side of the bed
paid the fare for everyone

drank from the cup without knowing what was in it
turned upside down till the blood rushed my head
wrote my dream through sleepfingers
put the dirty sheets back on the bed

held a silent interview with you
felt nothing and kept it to myself

corner store, no panties on
poured Drano in my coffee and milk down the sink
breezed past a proposal from a homeless man
dodged a viper I found in a poem
but came back with the poison still in me

Woke this morning with the fever finally broken
sickbed light sliced my dream in thirds
I was still travelling, visited
by old loves all night in my sleep
wasn't ready for the day, for the man right here
who woke up whispering *fucking amazing*
his spoon against the glass bowl
telling me *time to wake up* but I couldn't pull out
I was following ancient footprints
just about to find out three things I'd been wondering
& so returned—the stories I used to know by heart
pulling me from the vulnerable gifts: the morning
right under my nose, his peppermint shower smell
chasing after where my heart went:
back down the road, away from even this

A LITTLE STRANGER

And just as I had said I would,
just as I had done when alone—
I had stopped being careful.
I was sick of the tedium
of choose-the-right-words.
I left a memo for myself
describing how I would fail, and why.
Dear self, it read, you must make a plan.
You must carry your things and go.
This was never my strong suit, and thusly
I panicked and made myself a drink.
I sat in my lover's chair, my pride
wrapped around me like a grandmother blanket.
I took comfort in my old sad habits.
They would not love me
but at least they kept me safe.
They'd learned to grow themselves around me:
My same spot by the window, my side of the bed.
I couldn't change shape
for fear they wouldn't know me,
for fear I'd lose my holding patterns
and become a little stranger.

FLESH WOUND

I'd been thrown off, got star-dizzy from the fall;
hadn't quite been able to see and so grabbed hold
of the first thing I felt in the dark.
If it felt sturdy enough, if it could lift me—

As a wise man once said, seek and ye shall find.
I was human. And content.
But you, you made yourself go looking.
And me, that old eggshell feeling!

Don't give me your fears in a soundproof balloon,
I want them to hear what the truth can do.
Those accusations of infidelity about as true as childhood's
     cheese-moon—

Doesn't matter I guess, imagined hurt stings same as the
     real thing:
the belief and not the god that counts. Of course I stay true, but
what you go looking for, you'll find: those shades of betrayal!
As you wish: the infinite infidelities of the mind,
or eye, or careless tongue that lets out a little too much tell
     about a private thing.
What real betrayal looks like? It falls swiftly and severs the head.

Don't worry, Madame Guillotine will take grand care of me.
    But I've heard tell
an axed head's able to blink for three straight minutes before
    the lights snuff out for good.

BECAUSE IT WASN'T BROKEN

Like a disciple I followed the life of your hands
what they touched   what they didn't touch
how they flipped everything so the right side faced out

I wanted your hands to know me
but their skin grew calloused
around the knives they used the most

You had an urge to take everything apart
with a cat's paw or small blade cracking
small things into a second life

What was it that stopped you
from learning me   a place
     you didn't visit
     a place you couldn't fix

I held even your flaws in high regard
slowly and with difficulty in the habitual bed
bodies turned
with the good pain of a sleeping limb
needling awake
an ache in the back of the throat or deep
in the core's core   it had a fierceness to it
want and do-not-want   what it is I loved after
loved past   wondering if this counts
as one of the parts of me you wanted

you hid your mouth behind the blanket
but kept yourself
turned toward me—what was it in me that turned away
to give you the back of me, the last pieces I had,
my feet touching yours to warm them
you pushed against me, testing the waters
I wanted your hand at my throat
I pushed back   activating the old signals

the place I felt it start to happen almost hurt
your hands finding their way to the old places
your mouth at my neck I kept letting it happen, kept pushing
past the point where anybody would object
it was on the cusp forever and then the moment broke open
you pulled back from that fierceness—

this time not that hard place in you, cold
where I wanted and feared you
would fuck me with your hand on my throat—
instead slow and careful like
something in your hands
you didn't want to break

gently naked in a rush and you in me and I on top of you,
free because I was facing the wall, everything frenetic and
      the feeling
somewhere else until somewhere else until
nothing and I lay down beside you
watched sadness wash behind your face,
then sleep.

STATE OF EMERGENCY

Anywhere snow falls
becomes a temple.
An image draped in weather,
its silent white auspices that shatter.
The shape of a vehicle; the unbearable
silence inside it. The tires huddled
beneath its frame. White drifts
of weather fold it in: heavy,
pressed, a clover in a book.
Temporary. A prayer:
yes to wheels, to the idea of wheels,
they are the temple we have built,
the shrine to our god
which is leaving wherever we are.

VISITING

Your town was made of a quiet I had never felt
beside you on your wooden steps
held silent by a gratitude for so much sky

I started to tell you the story of home
my father and his leap across this country
with a courage sprung from losing
everything he made   with his two animal hands

After a while one shooting star showed itself
when I saw it my head went blank

Everything I would have wished for was already with me
your strong hand curled with mine
and the moon overseeing this small kindness

IN THE NIGHT FIELD

nervous, trying to figure
what it was the night wanted: drinking whiskey
        leaning on the old black gate,
black paint chipping, waiting for a boy,
getting too pretty—
small figure getting bigger

hello, human
a little trail
coming off the back of me
with fires in it
        bolder self I brought on like a cannon
        shot into the clover field and fizzling out soft

in that night field
horse tendons flexing   big energy there
would I fix my problem with more of the same problem
yes

TO THE RIVER HOUSE

recurring dream

It happened every night in pieces: you left me
talismans from the other side, dreamthings
with a sideways-sense that blurred
when I went to back away. You were tethered in place,
sunk in the mud near a threadbare bench,
your tired eaves, your yellow face whose windows
watched the river slap at the banks when the boats went by.

I was driving away from you, my eye
on the rearview. I watched your trees recede
into a green hum, your yellow behind me and behind me
till something gave like floodwater:
a long thread unraveling.
A feeling in the hands
like braiding hair.

Now I look at my life
with a seasonal madness,
frantic at what I left behind:
banana plants with brown edges
that curled like hair, old photographs
we pulled from the wall. Those white squares
where the frames had been.

ROAD TRIP

Driving home in a cloud of highway rain,
this landscape aches like a bruise, barred-in
by black fences that hold out the road,
that lift and unravel the shape of my life:

Oldham Acres, Riverside, my ribs
clasp tight, my father's place
looms in a sycamore thicket:

America, Kentucky, I take
my place, a story I can't stop telling:
Pignut, Catalpa, Buckeye, and Hickory

river sheen   horse mane the color of me
my apple in his teeth   his snot on my sleeve
down here   we get what we need

BELATED BIRTHDAY POEM

for my father

You're two thousand miles away
with your Hawaiian shirt and White Russian in hand
at your Big Lebowski-themed birthday bowling event,
and I'm stuck on the other edge of the world swatting fruit flies,
the health inspector's stink-eye rising behind the
    clipboard—

but you, I heard yesterday you caught the sun
trying to extinguish itself, sliding down
into the ridiculous Pacific: you asked the sun
what's not to live for? It hissed under its breath
and then the lights went out. Fine. Today pairs best
with words like fulcrum, maps of arctic places,
and the two overripe bananas I let go brown
in a paper bag, thinking past the rotten parts
to the bread I'll make for you that's sweet, and rises.

HEIRLOOM ELEGY

News of my grandfather came in spirals
through the telephone: time of death
8:28, a palindrome I took my comfort in

We go forward and backward
to me he was a black lung sleeping stone giant
spiders up his legs and a severance in his heart

his apartment   TV stand and dark armchair
alone and stale in it

Lieutenant
his silence   made of cherry pie and whiskey
anything but those dead boys

and dying himself, he tried to take my father with him
pleading *help me*
with the look of a man who knows better

Souvenir:
his conquest got him a Purple Heart
and a pile of dead soldiers in the family crypt, saying
you put us here
now put us to rest

Now I am grown
and reject anything   that will give us more ghosts
Years later, driving between my two places
taking Byrum things away from my mother's garage,
his rifle and his folded flag, blood-stained helmet
with a German name carved in it: Heinrich—
our legacy of engravers—
weird relics of an old war I carried
those miles back home

good morning radio signal, brought to you by the dream I
    half-remembered
        this morning I was falling back   writing it down
the pen in my hand tipping back into—something about a
    textile mill
you and I were walking toward in uniform, the image
    yellowing at the edges
my dream amnesia   kinky merchandise I borrow from
    myself
        hallelujah, inescapably
last night a man's voice wrapped around the inside of my head:
"you don't have to complicate it, just—bring it!"

INFINITY, CHICAGO, THE BIGGEST POSSIBLE SKY

for Fell & Kinser

On the hotel's quilted bed
Adam reclines, eating cookies
in the late Etruscan style

At dinner with friends I fall out of myself
I go out the window to mingle with stars
in love with long distance:
learn how far I can get
from the seat of myself
and still tether
by the skin of my teeth
this sky goes forever   I'm tinier here
can't stop laughing at all this disaster
can't stop flickering off like a hurricane lamp

Adam's on my left, scribbling poems on a napkin
"poetry is a team sport"
no I in it
fine, I'm tired enough to let myself be carried

Kinser's eyes go homesick
Nantahala sparkles in them
Red sediment sister   head full of mica flecks

that river   asking after me
I want all of you in my corner forever
can't wait to see you
belligerent in the afterlife

Please say you'll meet me at the hotel bar

Every day you move farther outside
the outlines kinder   more dangerous
a little darker now

      and winter. Trees
      blacker: brittle white paper sky
      that no longer holds you.

Having come this far
still knowing nothing
      where will you be going

and if you have arrived already
tell me who sits beside you
who will show you kindness and
      who will the others be.

ONCE AGAIN THE WORLD ABSCONDS WITH MY BELONGINGS

I picture a Warehouse of Byrum
lit in bad fluorescents
filled with wallets, orphan keys

map with my places circled
gift I bought but never gave
T-shirt I kept when he left

items gently filed away
by a cartoon hand
who labels each thing

"to let go"
"to let go"
"to let go"

YEAR IN REVIEW

"It's possible that I still live there"

— Alice Notley, "101"

On the porch back home
I sat missing him.
Listening to the rain hiss.

After 2600 miles, a blizzard,
three planes and a bus
to get back to me,
he collapses on my doorstep
exhausted and full of something
he could no longer withhold:
Colorado in his vowels,
that mountain howl.
His snow boots dripping in the hall.

We negotiate: we tear down walls
paint over old colors

he gets stronger
his calluses come back

but even when he comes home
he doesn't come home

Independence Day

We give our best selves over
to a rooftop and a six-pack of beer

he is standing in the sun on the other side
smiling at everyone else

when the sky starts its colors again
last year explodes underneath this one:
the wreckage of small autonomies

on a different roof, love and a bottle of whiskey between us
side by side but looking out at fireworks across the river
knowing he was already out there with them

August

A low roar
and the fan turns away again. Hot.
How long will I abide
this moving toward and away,
these surges and retreats—
from mornings when you walk in singing to
how long can I stand the back of you

sleeping
or walking
always a few paces out in front.

Now I live here
in your habits
tracks and signs
in an empty room:

Wet towel on the back of the door.
Wet footprints that evaporate on the hardwood floor.

Stiff in my dress
holding a bad truth

should leave : can't leave ::

October

Most of the time
I'm alone in the house
in front of a screen
in front of a bar
or behind one
facing friends
or the back of you sleeping

I press your spine
like I'm on a city bus
and the next stop's mine

Outside, shoes whiten on power lines
delicate ribbons of snow
knot around a streetlight

If you let your eyes go soft
barbed wire turns to white cursive
looping fences

When the wind dies down
the snow lifts up and waits
like a patient man

when the woman he loves
is storming. Just letting it be. Gusts again
and the snow streams down like hair.

When a man drifts up
against the side of a woman
like snow and she is storming

and cold seeps through the floorboards
and nothing in it
that isn't lonely.

Christmas

Morning when my hands are a question
he doesn't want to answer

When I push against the walls that make us possible:
this relationship brought to you by
a conditional alliance
held together by silence

"Well, I'm not happy with—this"
he waves his hand in a wide arc
and he is pointing to everything

the books I loved, their pages
with his fingerprints

coffee table
we stained together
spice cabinet
sanded down
his sweat in it

fine so
burn it down

Birthday

I can barely see out from under the hood of my winter coat
but I notice him I check my impulse to fear I calm myself
down for the third time today don't be afraid just a neighbor
walking home like me but anyone can see vulnerable written
all over my face walking in a fog of unfortunate events
another one starts without me it keeps being about to happen
he is looking at me from the corners of his eyes I see
his hood raise up he crosses the street in the middle of
the block he is behind me in this slow pursuit I cross
the street he crosses the street I cross the street it takes
forever I don't want to run afraid to make it worse
up ahead a bodega's lit sign the neon lights chase each other
around its border I think I can get there when I am close
enough to see it's not a bodega it's a tire store and it's closed
it is already too late his fists and stars explode in the back
of my brain and I am on my knees beside two parked

trucks blocked from view of anyone who might save me

he is telling me to shut the fuck up and no one hears but

lucky traffic a gypsy cab rolls by and he runs off I stumble

my hand outstretched and blood on my mouth did you

see his face the driver asks and what about the other one

what yes you know two men ran away I can't—he hands

me his cell phone and the neon buttons are crawling like

worms I can't—can you call I can't work your phone and

we drive in circles around the block we find them again the

headlights sweep white over their faces they had dropped

my bag everything in it smashed against a brick wall

the cops come and their red and blue wash over my face

In the Bath

he puts his hand on me

I come to
in its outline
I spit blood

small white tiles

in the corner
a dead spider
is clenched like a fist

sloped porcelain
where shampoo bottles
totter on the ledge

a sliver of soap
grafted on
to another bar of soap

no reflection
just a fog on the mirror
hello

he gets in with me
behind the white curtain.

I curl over
my knees
so as to not be seen.

he reaches out
to wash my back.

we sit there silent
till the water goes cold
in pockets like a lake.

Then he was gone.

I stayed home alone
with my back against
the innermost wall.

February 28, 8:15 a.m.

Something turns over.

something upstairs ignites
something smells a little off
something in the architecture splinters

morning steps out of its shadow
just a little left of center

and I wake up.

Let me try to tell you how it happened:

another day waking up in our bed

with the slow painful remembering

that morning had become

no alarm today, instead, this:

too early, still groggy, half-dreaming

in the feeling of water, a burning smell

and the racket of hoses

that scatters the dream-fog to show

it's real: water pouring down

from the ceiling light I read by,

coming down in brown ribbons

to pool on my body in the bed:

rivers from the ceiling where it buckled at a crack

I'd spent a year staring into, wishing you home.

The walls had been saying what I already knew.
but my life had taught me to listen in rivers—

how to tell you:
how the water
kept coming
I was trying
to catch it
in a bucket
like a keepsake

I pull on my boots
and go to stand with the others
in pajamas on the sidewalk
and we watch it burn.

When they said it was over
I went back into the room.

The ceiling hung open
                showing its pink asbestos insides
                like cotton candy
they warned me not to touch.

The power out.

The afternoon light threw its long shadows
on the books
whose pages warped from the water

which hadn't quite washed clean
the chalkboard on the wall
where I couldn't find the heart to fully erase
the note you wrote
to the old me.

No one knocked anymore.
And no point in locking the door.

But I kept returning.

Kept watch with my surrogate eye:
the part of me that was glad to see it go.

The men that came said
these walls can't stay.

It was true: they showed me where
they'd rotted through.

1G

A red apartment whose hallway always smelled like piss and
    curry.
As long as we lived there I could never sleep
because of noise from the street: strings of profanity
that sailed through my bedroom window
and exploded inside my dream.

The lady upstairs and her elderly mother
who was nearly deaf and always in the bath:
they kept the TV on full blast
and sometimes on my bad days
the sounds from her shows
felt more real to me than I did to myself
and louder, so I would give up
trying to write or think
and just listen to their tin-can voices
worming in, muffled, through the ceiling vents.

The one-eyed super named Johnson
who called me 1-G like it was my name:
after the fire
when so many strangers came in and out
through the plastic sheet taped over my door
which I stopped bothering to lock
he stole a bag of quarters I used for our laundry
and a poster I'd pulled from our bedroom wall
diagramming the anatomy of a human skeleton.

Later when I came to collect my mail from his apartment
I found these things and a few others, which he pretended
to have been keeping safe for me.

Claim

one green couch where your ghost was still sleeping
one kitchen table with your fingerprints rinsed away
one lamp I kept burning
one framed fabric scrap
blue with gingko leaves

the books I loved
their wet pages

coffee table
we stained together
spice cabinet
sanded down

gone.

I rewound the tapes. I watched the old footage again, then
    tried it in reverse:
the tattoo un-inked itself and the fists unclenched inside
    their pockets.
Whole chunks of burnt plaster leapt up and clung to the
    ceiling.
The posters curled back up the wall, the books spit firewater
    at the neighbors upstairs,
and my bed kindly made itself so, returning, I'd feel nothing
    vital had been broken.

The plane I'd fled on flew backwards and my hair streamed
    out in front of me.
Whole poems erased themselves: I couldn't quite think what
    made me itch
for a pen to begin with. The mail returned itself to sender
    and my old love was there.
His hand un-smoothed the hair from my forehead, the lock
    fell back in place,
and I couldn't see anything past it. I didn't know then, and
    still don't, what's beyond it.

NOTES & ACKNOWLEDGMENTS

My gratitude to the following journals where these poems appeared in fledgling states: *The Bakery*; *Bodega Magazine*; *Forklift, Ohio*; *Ghost Town*; *H_NGM_N*; *Handsome Journal*; *La Fovea*; *Pine Hills Review*; *Poor Claudia: Phenome*; *Split Lip Magazine*

***

"Big Buck Hunter" owes Hank's Saloon in Brooklyn a shot of whiskey.

"In Footprints" borrows lines from Jean Valentine's poem "Dufy Postcard."

"Model Airplane" is for my grandfather, Thomas Walter Pelle.

"Road Trip (Train landscape)" gives a nod to Thomas Sayers Ellis.

"At the End of the Highline" is for Gabe Kruis.

"Heirloom Elegy" is for my grandfather, Raymond C. Byrum.

***

Thank you to the faculty and students of the MFA program at Hunter College, and to the staff and fellow residents of the Vermont Studio Center, where many of these poems were written.

Thanks to Catherine Barnett and Tom Sleigh for their kind words about this book.

Matt Hart, Eric Appleby, Tricia Suit, Amanda Smeltz, and Nate Pritts: big love for your eyes, ears, and endless patience.

ABOUT THE AUTHOR

Katie Byrum is a native Kentuckian who currently lives in Brooklyn, New York. For sixteen years, she has worked in the food and beverage industry, studying whiskey and its effects on the human psyche. She co-curates two poetry events in Brooklyn, the witchy series COVEN and the Tri-Lengua Reading Series.

Her work has been featured in *Gulf Coast Magazine, Lumberyard, Big Bell, iO Poetry, Split Lip Magazine, Ghost Town, Pine Hills Review, H_NGM_N, Forklift, Ohio, Handsome, Poor Claudia: Phenome,* and elsewhere.

Visit her online at **hellohumanblog.tumblr.com.**

CPSIA information can be obtained
at www.ICGtesting.com
Printed in the USA
FFOW03n1322141215
19650FF